The Don't Laugh Challenge™

Second Edition

PRIZES!

STOP

$50 GIFT CARD

Think YOU can win our JOKE CONTEST?!?!

The Don't Laugh Challenge is having a CONTEST to see who is the MOST HILARIOUS boy or girl in the USA.

Please have your parents email us your best **original** joke and you could win a $50 gift card to Amazon.

Here are the rules:

1. It must be funny. Please do not give us jokes that aren't funny. We get enough of those from our joke writers

2. It must be original. We have computers and we know how to use them.

3. No help from the parents. Plus, they aren't even that funny anyway!!

Email your best joke to:
 ### Bacchuspublish@gmail.com

Winners will be announced via email.

Bacchus Publishing House

The Don't Laugh Challenge™
Instructions:

- Sit down facing your opponent at eye level.

- Take turns reading jokes to each other.

- First person to make the opponent laugh, wins a point!

- First person to 3 points wins & is crowned The Don't Laugh MASTER.

Game on!

QUESTION & ANSWER
JOKES

Why is a shallow beach so hot?

Because of all the microwaves

How do you light up a tennis court?

With a tennis match.

Why did the astronaut leave his wife?

He needed space.

What superhero can you sit on and also leads meetings?

The Chairman.

How can you tell the difference between a male and female chromosome?

Pull down its genes.

Why are automobiles, good listeners?

They've got great engin-eers.

Why did the chef get fired?

He was being too salty with the customers.

Did you hear about the astronaut that couldn't pay attention?

He was spaced out.

What do you get if you leave your dog out in the snow?

A puppsicle.

Why was the stadium full of water?

Somebody turned the floodlights on.

What's a duck's favorite snack?

Quackers

Why didn't the comedian make jokes about armored vehicles?

They always tank.

Why do hats make good scouts?

They always go on ahead.

Why should you avoid boring bankers?

They lose your interest.

What do you get when you mix a balloon and a fountain drink?

Soda Pop.

Did you hear about the bad behaved Math book?

It had a lot of problems.

What's the best key to open a banana?

A monkey.

Why didn't the snow plow driver take things seriously?

Because there was snow problem.

What's a prisoner favorite game?

Trouble

Why did the pencil smell?

It was a No.2

Did you hear about the man who got
struck by lighting?

He was shocked.

Why does jumping on a trampoline end winter?

It becomes springtime.

What type of fish goes great with peanut butter?

A jellyfish

Why is it hard to play cards on a boat?

Because someone's always sitting on the deck.

Why was the belt in prison?

For holding up trousers.

What did the feet say to the socks?

"I'm sorry, but it socks to be you"

Where do people grow medicine?

In a farmacy.

How do you fire somebody in a shoe shop?

You give them the boot.

How do you guarantee your kids will grow up ugly?

Ask your mom!

What did the hamburger call his daughter?

Patty.

Where does a monkey go to get his workout on?

A jungle gym.

Why is prison full of salesmen?

It's full of hard cells.

How do armies choose their leaders?

At the general election.

What's the cheapest way to buy 4 suits?

Buy a pack of cards.

What do you call a Dinosaur in a cowboy hat?

Tyrannosaurus Tex.

What do you do if someone says "sticks and stones may break my bones, but words will never hurt me"?

Hit'em with a dictionary.

Why is tennis noisy?

All the rackets

Did you hear about the strawberry and blueberry that started a band?

They jammed!

Why are golfers party animals?

They know where all the clubs are.

Did you hear about the annoying ant?

He bugged everyone

Why does the president always measure up?

Because he's the ruler.

What should you say if your mom wants to discuss your underwear?

"Keep it brief."

Did you hear about the cellphone that was playing hard to get?

It was giving mixed signals.

Why did the bad pirate have to stroll around town with a big piece of wood?

He was sentenced to walk the plank.

What happens if you fence with somebody unarmed?

You won't get the point.

Did you hear about the bird that was afraid to fly?

It was a chicken

Why did the math tutor open a furniture store?

She had so many multiplication tables.

Why did the pupil eat his homework?

His tutor said it was a piece of cake.

Why didn't the two magnets date?

They find themselves repulsive.

Did you hear about the water that was angry?

It was steaming!

Did you hear about the popular bee?

He was all the buzz!

How do trains sneeze?

Ah-choo choo

Why was the pumpkin winning so much?

It was on a roll.

What are zombies favorite birds?

Craaaaaaanes

How did the jack-o-lantern feel after it was complimented?

It was glowing.

Why do werewolves not like clouds?

They have a silver lining.

Why can't apples go trick or treating?

They always get spoiled.

Why did no one want to play the zombie soccer team?

They're stuff competition.

What is a witches favorite thing to learn in school?

Spelling.

What do you call a bee that learned magic?

Bee witched.

How did the witches hat win the argument?

It made a good point.

Why did the witches broom have such a big ego?

It couldn't stay grounded.

Why don't mummies eat sandwiches?

They prefer wraps.

What place did the vampire come in during the race?

Dead last.

How do pumpkins always stay such good friends?

They always patch things up.

What do banana peels say on Halloween?

Trip or treat.

Why didn't the pumpkin want to go to the movie?

It heard it was a smash hit.

Why didn't the skeleton concert go very well?

It was a pretty thin crowd.

What did the lightbulb go as for Halloween?

Flash.

Why are pumpkins afraid of calendars and heights?

They never make it past the fall.

What part of the job do skeletons hate?

Breaks.

What is the best vegetable on Halloween?

Candy corn.

What did the knife go as for Halloween?

A dino-sword.

What's a golfer's favorite number?

Fooooooooour!

Why did the surfer swim back to shore?

He couldn't wave good-bye.

Why did Dr. Frankenstein sew his monster's head closed at the laundromat?

To keep him from getting brainwashed.

What is the worst type of cup to pour hot tea into?

A buttercup.

When Dave drove to work, it never cost him money. Why?

He used the freeway.

What happens when you use spot remover on a leopard?

Nothing. A leopard can't change its spots and neither can you!

What can you say about Paul and Pat when they squeezed into the tiny space craft?

They were like two P's in a pod!

Where is the best place to sit when a submarine is diving?

Inside.

Why did the lawyer show up in court in his underwear?

He forgot his lawsuit!

What is the nun's favorite toy to play with?

A praydough.

Why didn't the hammerhead shark feel well?

His head was pounding.

Why did the yeast stop telling jokes to the bread?

He couldn't get a rise out of her.

Which day of the week does 3 follow?

Twosday.

For which crimes are cats most known?

Kitty littering.

Why can you have tea for two or even three, but not four?

Four starts with the letter "F."

Why do actions speak louder than words?

Words can't speak!

What should you do if you bite off more than you can chew?

Spit it out.

Why are geologists trying to mine clouds?

Every cloud has a silver lining.

Why was Alexander Graham's invention of the telephone a waste of time?

He could have heard everything through the grapevine!

Which is the happiest capital in the U.S.?

Annapolis, the capital of MERRY-LAND!

How do you know when a snake is upset?

It gets hiss-terical.

Why did the knight use poison instead of his sword to kill the mythical winged, fire-breathing creature?

He didn't want the fight to drag-on.

Why isn't "Werewolf" spelled with an "H"?

No one wants to scream "Herewolf"!

What does a corn spider spin?

Cobwebs.

What is a tree's favorite drink?

Root beer.

When the camel asked for sugar with
his tea, what did the waitress ask?

"One hump or two?"

Which animal loves the Pansy flower?

Chimpanzee!

KNOCK- KNOCK
JOKES

Knock knock
Who's there?
Robin
Robin who?
Robin you! Give me all your money!

Knock Knock
Who's there?
Luke
Luke who?
Luke through the window and see for
yourself

Knock knock
Who's there?
Phil
Phil who?
Phil me in why you're not opening the door.

Knock knock
Who's there?
Taylor
Taylor who?
Taylor my pants, please! They're ripped!

Knock knock
Who's there?
Wind
Wind who?
I'm not climbing in the window!! Open the door!

Knock knock
Who's there?
Russian
Russian who?
Russian, you to finish the joke!

Knock knock
Who's there?
Sam who?
Sam person it was yesterday let me in.

Knock knock
Who's there?
Donwanna
Donwanna who?
Donwanna tell you, but let me in any way!

Knock knock
Who's there?
Honeybee.
Honeybee, who?
Honeybee a dear and get my tea!

Knock knock
Who's there?
Noah
Noah who?
Noah good reason why you won't open the
door?

Knock knock
Who's there?
Weave
Weave who?
Weave got to weave this basket!

Knock knock
Who's there
Sadie
Sadie who?
Sadie password and I let you in.

Knock knock
Who's there?
Otto.
Otto, who?
Otto correct keeps changing my texts!

Knock knock
Who's there?
Cash
Cash who?
Cashews? You gotta be nuts!

Knock Knock
Who's there?
Iferr
Iferr who?
Iferr got what I was going to say.

Knock knock
Who's there?
Luke
Luke who?
Luke who came to see you!

Knock knock
Who's there?
My fell
My fell who?
My fell who American, let me in.

Knock knock
Who's there?
Claire
Claire who?
Clairely you don't remember me!

Knock knock
Who's there?
Amish
Amish who?
Amish you too now let me in!

RIDDLES

What school do you have to drop out to graduate from?

A parachute school.

What's the lightest thing you can only hold briefly?

Your breath

What's stuck in place but travels the world?

A Stamp

What is the world's quietest
four-man rock group?

Mount Rushmore

What kind of driver has no arms or
legs?

A Screwdriver

Who follows you around all day, but
never at night?

Your shadow

What lies on its back 100 feet in the air?

A dead centipede

Why did the table go to the doctors?

It broke its legs

What has two hands but can't clap?

A clock

What can say words loudly but cannot speak?

An echo

What has no nose but still smells?

A bathroom

What type of castle can be destroyed by water?

A sand castle

What kind of coat can only be put on wet?

Paint

Despite my name, I am not very fast. One step in me might be your last! What am I?

Quick sand

My bed is full of rocks and may be wet. Not to mention full of fish! What am I?

A river

I can be mistaken for an ocean, Though I contain no water. I often follow the letter B, But compared to me, F is hotter. What am I?

The letter "C"

I may have a tail or two, or maybe none at all, when I plan on going to, a fancy social ball. What am I?

Girl with a pony tail

I'm not related to the cute and furry rabbit, even though you chase me from household habit. Using air currents as my guide, under beds and dressers I shall hide. What am I?

Dust Bunny

While I look like a ribbon, I am bigger than a tent. Colorful as I am, for wrapping, I'm not mean. What am I?

Rainbow

I have a nose and two wings and more than one back seat. Go ahead, dive from me, and land on both feet. What am I?

An airplane

TONGUE TWISTERS

1. Mary may make major mall mail magic.

2. Black bleek babes busting blueberries.

3. Parents pack painters pads for park pages.

4. Dazzled dad dangers dance dares daily.

5. Lazy lady lawyer labels law lands last.

6. Sacrifice salt savings for salad sales samples.

7. Variety varies valued vacations vastly.

8. Yet yellow yarn yells yesterday yearly.

9. Obey odd offers on officers opposite orders.

10. Capable camps can't capture captains carefully.

11. Bad bison balance behind big barbers badly.

12. Account accidents accept access across academies.

13. Keen kickers kiss kitchen keys kindly.

14. Jason the jealous jokester judged jets judgement.

15. Uncles undo uni umbrellas under union.

16. Queens quality quiz qualifies quick quotation quarterly.

17. Few festival females feel fear feeling.

18. Wishy Washy Washing Wipers wished for willows

19. Wentz Went Once Step

20. Buzzy bee buzzed blankly in Burt's baggage

21. Witches Wishes Witches Wishes Witches Wishes

22. Wallie Waited While He Ollied

23. Number Two owned two tutus

24. The bow tie tied the dyed bow tie

25. The Boxer Boxed the Foxy Fox

31. The Cook Took the Cook Book

32. The Bee in the Tree Buzzed Politely to the other Bees in the Tree.

33. Picky Peter Picked Apart the Broken Part.

34. Misses Swishes Washes Dishes

35. We Plea Quietly to the Bumble Bee

36. Take the Plate off the Roller Skates

37. Eight Mates Ate Apple Cakes

38. Sixty-seven servants sat on seven straws on Sunday

39. Chester the cheetah got caught cheating in checkers and chess

40. Waves whisper wishing words to wise wishers

41. Ace the Apple ate all the apricots accidently

42. Cooks cook crepes with crunchy cookies

43. Sammy shunned his silly sister Sadie.

44. Fred, Ted, and Ed went to bed instead of read

45. Fred fed his friend for fifty feeds

46. Tammy took a tasty look at twenty Twinkies

47. Alright, the Knight road into the night tonight

48. The fish flipped from feeling fishy

49. The prickly pear couldn't pair with peoples parties

50. The stairs stared at the silver stars silently

Made in the USA
Las Vegas, NV
04 October 2022

56400510R00046